The Altar Boy

By

Sean Brennan

Without any discussion, in fifth grade, you became an altar boy. There were few ways in which an eleven-year-old could attain status at St. Edmund School in Oak Park, and altar boy was at the top of the list. You could also choose to be a crossing guard and wear the shiny, orange belt around your waist and the strap that ran from shoulder to hip, and help the little ones cross the streets. You could be in the band and learn to clang an instrument or join the choir and sing to the angels, or get really daft and help the nuns on Saturdays, but nothing held the high esteem of donning a red cassock that ran from shoulder to toe and a white, lacy surplice that cloaked the cassock, and then go parading before the altar with the priest, to kneel in front of the tabernacle and otherwise direct a Catholic's most treasured rite: the Mass.

The priest would come over to school every eight weeks and hand out report cards. When he entered, the room would fall deathly silent except for a few of the girl's irrepressible giggling, "Oh, he's so handsome." The presence that the priest commanded was enthralling. Sometimes you thought you were looking at God. And who could ignore an audience with him? The priest would stand at the front of the room and call out each kid's name, peruse the report card to examine your progress, and then offer a critique as he handed you your grades.

"Excellent work," to the smart kids.

"You're better than this," to the so-so kids.

"Needs a little work," to the not so-so kids.

And to the Bradley's, the slackers, the kids who were never going to get it and didn't care, "Make sure you show this to your mother." But their mothers didn't care either.

And when the cards had all been passed out, and with them a dose of glee to some, humiliation to others, the priest would belt out, "Are there any volunteers to become an altar boy?" This was an invitation from the priest, the closest thing to God on this Earth, to stand with him on the altar in front of the congregation and look proud and solemn. Every boy's hand in the room went sky-high in response, except Bradley's. Bradley was looking out the window; he couldn't care less. The girls sat, bored and neglected, knowing that only the lads could serve God: There were no altar girls. Some thought being an altar boy was the first step to the priesthood, and every Irish family yearned to have one...a priest, that is. A generation ago, my father, Pops, was the priest designate for his family and enthusiastically entered the seminary. My cousin Paddleboat was the chosen one in his.

When you joined the seminary, the Church sequestered you from mainstream society as a way to assert complete control and keep you from all the worldly temptations. The biggest temptation was girls, and you know what that meant. Sex was forbidden, and if Jesus didn't have any, neither should you. They didn't even want you to want it. That was a sin, too, and lowered you to the level of the Protestants and anyone else who appreciated a good-looking woman.

The Church hadn't planned on my mother, Bridie, showing up, fresh from Cloonmore in Eire, with her rich brogue and direct blue gaze. She cast a spell on the unsuspecting seminarian and ruined the script. Pops' instincts took over, and he succumbed to the temptations of the tall, Irish farm-girl immigrant with the fine mane of thick, brown hair and 'a way about her.' It was Bridie who ruined the plan, the one that God had laid out for Pops. And could you blame the poor lad?

So, six years into the seminary, Pops succumbed to Bridie's lure and sneaked out the back door, incurring the wrath of his family and the Bishop, too. The ascendancy didn't like losing recruits. Pops was ostracized by his whole clan who were incensed that someone had the gall to reject "God's calling." That's what they called it to make you believe that you didn't have any choice. If you bought that malarkey you might actually stay in the seminary for a while, ignoring your own instincts, which came hourly when you were a teenager.

Pops lost everything when he bolted—guaranteed salvation, a scripted future and being the closest thing to God that a human could be—but he got Bridie. *Nice trade, Pops.* He was damned and ostracized and left on an island for a few years, a disgrace to the family. But that didn't stop him. Pops wasn't one to be intimidated. Exoneration finally came years later. You see, Bridie and Pops saw enough of each other to add eleven new faces to the parish enrollments.

The Church loved numbers of worshippers and their monetary contributions, too—perhaps even more than they loved enlisting new priests. The pastor was always prospecting for new seminarians or altar boys asking often, "Do you have the calling?" You always said, "Yes," because you couldn't say, "No," to him. He was smart enough to never ask Murphy or Turk or Bradley because he couldn't count on their answers, and their pedigrees were lacking. But I saw the perks: You gained some status when you became an altar boy and the extra cash helped too with the way our portfolios were looking.

I could forecast the pinnacles of altar boyhood: attending the annual Altar Boy Picnic—a sports outing that let you have a full day out of the cage—and the greatest glory of all: the possibility of playing a key role at the Christmas Eve Mass. All this promised some money, time off from school, and more than a little glory. My hand flew up, along with most of the other boys. So I became an altar boy, inching my way closer to God and heaven.

"Tomorrow after school for the first practice," the priest announced. By the next day, half the volunteers had thought better of waking up early for Sunday morning services and neglected to show up for the altar boy rehearsals. I showed up—the perks were too irresistible. Within months, I became an old veteran at serving, ringing the bells, swinging the incense, lighting the candles, carrying the cross. In a weak moment Sister Michael, the principal, made me head of the fifth grade altar boys. It was a huge honor to preside over God's little servants, and it got you out of school too. Sister Michael's motives were unclear, but I think that she had a soft spot in her heart for the less fortunate candidates who were an unlikely choice for a position usually assigned to the doctors' and dentists' sons.

Sister Michael knew that she was taking a risk putting me at the head, but her plan was to shame me into conformity. "Don't let me down," she said, adding more pressure and angst.

Our Altar Boy careers began engulfed in an angelic aura. It was lofty status assisting the priests in bringing Mass and the Eucharist to the congregation. The night before I served, Bridie would make sure I was well scrubbed and my hair combed before she sent me off to serve God. Crisply garbed in starched cassocks and lace over garments, my cherubic face would gleam under the altar lights and flickering candles. We wore red for happy Masses and black for sad ones. Our duties were crucial and varied. We prepared the cruets, full of the wine and water that, when blended, became the blood of Jesus. We rang the chimes at the critical parts of the Mass; timing and touch were required. At funerals, the short guys would carry the candles, and the tall guys would carry the crucifix. We'd swing the silver thurible, a container that housed the incense, and send a good plume of smoke over the coffins and relics. At communion, that's when the priest laid a thin wafer on your tongue, the Body of Christ, we'd hold the patens, a small silver plate, under the recipient's chin just in case the host went wayward. The worst part of our job was looking down everyone's throat and at their spotted and discolored tongues wondering what the hell they ate yesterday.

To the boys in our neighborhood who hadn't slept in, we'd give a wink and press the paten to their throats, basking in our power as Jesus was laid on their tongues. No moment was so sacred that we couldn't inject some kind of mischief. But we were always required to look solemn and serene. There was no smiling. That was how Mass was: solemn and dour. The more somber you looked the holier you were, and most hammed it up pretty well. Murphy would be in heaven if God couldn't recognize a faker. Your solemnity started the moment you walked into church. In moments, you'd go from screeching and laughter on the lawn in front of church to more solemn and more somber with each step as you climbed toward the church's front gates. Once inside the front door, the curtain was totally drawn, and complete silence was required. The only snickers you'd hear were when Murphy snapped the hat-clip on the back of the pew and sent a crack echoing through the church. The nun would come from behind as the crack slowly faded into the nave and she'd look down each pew searching for the culprit. The only evidence was the giggling that followed, but everyone was doing that so most times the crime went unpunished. It was the height of frustration for a nun…witnessing a trespass and being powerless.

The chimes would sound, *ding dong ding*, and from the sacristy, the hidden room behind the altar where the secrets were kept, the priest would emerge garbed in flowing robes, looking like Jesus would have if he'd had money, and flanked by an altar boy on each arm. The silence and solemnity would deepen as the priest slowly walked to the front of the altar, raised both arms to the sky and God, and let out a chant in Latin. And for the next hour the altar boys had to pretend that we were paying attention, which we weren't. The kids in the pews only looked straight ahead for fear the nun behind them would sense their indifference and come up behind and clip them one. The whole exercise was painful, and we didn't much understand what it was all about, only that painful stuff made you better. Pain was at the core of every process.

The sermons were always about how sinful you were and how you needed to be more like Jesus. Often, as I was perched on the altar playing altar boy, looking out at the drawn faces, I'd wonder why this couldn't be like the Black churches, hoppin' and boppin'. No one was having fun in our church, and no one was supposed to. This was church, dammit, your weekly commitment that kept you out of hell.

When Mass was over and when you weren't serving, just after the final blessing that gave you one last injection of goodness, you'd start to file out of your pews. You'd be so eager to leave, you'd knock into the person in front of you so you could get outside and feel life again. When I'd take my first step outside, I'd breathe deeply and go charging down the steps, taking two at a time and the last three in one lunging jump, knowing that the next dreaded holy hour was a good seven long days away.

All this was somewhat balanced by some major payoffs for being an altar boy. One perk was serving early Mass at the local hospital where they gave you a full buffet breakfast. The buffet ranked high because you got to eat as much bacon, doughnuts, scrambled eggs and pancakes as you could possibly stuff inside yourself in one morning. The buffet had all the things we never had at home, and boy, were we hungry. The hospital lost on this one, especially when we served.

It was a real trip at the hospital. The chapel was empty because most of the people who were supposed to be there were upstairs dying. The priest was Father Duffacy, who seemed like he was a hundred years old. At six feet two and 120 pounds his profile was hard to spot. They kept a bed open for him just in case…you never knew when. He walked by inches, not steps, and when he genuflected the cartilage in his knees would pop and fill the chapel with gunshot sounds. I ducked the first time I heard one. He couldn't talk anymore, only mumble, but halfway through the Mass, he'd raise his voice and you'd hear a, "Haila the Mary Fullo the Grace," and everyone present would be cleansed of their sins and the Mass official. It wasn't long before we lost the hospital duty…something about, "We can't afford these guys anymore."

But the Altar Boy Picnic was the really special perk: we got a whole day off from school, got to wear plain clothes and play baseball, and got to leave the uncommitted boys behind with all the undeserving girls, who couldn't go because they weren't good enough to serve the Lord. We got to ride in a big

yellow school bus and spend the day at Pottawattamie
Park where we could run, play, slide, swing and swim
until we couldn't stand anymore. It was the highlight
of our year and the payoff that made all those Masses
worth it. The Altar Boy Picnic was our yearly vacation
packed into one glorious day. The bus ride was a trek
of just a few miles but, in our minds, a journey to
heaven. It was the day when you got to show up to
school in a sweatshirt and jeans, punching the
padding out of your baseball glove, if it even had any,
and dreaming of pure joy without one nun to say no
to you or tell you what to do or remind you of your
shortcomings. It was nunvana...*er, nirvana.*

Anticipation built as the day of the picnic
approached. I had no reason to sense the disaster
ahead. The day of the picnic was chilly, but there was
no rain, at least, not yet. My newspaper route was
done, and my excitement grew as I pulled on my
worn blue jeans and White Sox sweatshirt and laced
up my gym shoes. Bridie bid me *adieu* at the back
screen door, barking out "be carefuls" and stuffing a

strip of sheet, in lieu of a cotton hanky, in my pocket for the inevitable "shnotters" that you'd get on a chilly day. At the last minute, she asked, "And your jockeys?" Her primal fear was that you'd be in an accident and as you were being undressed in the emergency room the doctor wouldn't find any or discover a *smather* that needed attention. The old screen door, with its holes and rips, slammed as I took the last three stairs in one leap. I looked back and could see Bridie waving.

"Be a gentleman," she warned.

As I continued my mad dash for the alley and my road to ecstasy, I looked over my shoulders and yelled back to Bridie, "Ma, I forgot. How'd the tea leaves look?" Apart from her other powers, my mother was a psychic and could read the tea leaves and predict the future.

"A bit muddled today. There was a wayward clump that could either be sunshine or a big cloud. Be careful," she warned one more time.

"Muddled…" I thought. That wasn't like her to be evasive the day of a trip or not find some silver cloud in the residue. I hesitated at the back of the garage and thought about a second reading to clarify things and then heard Mahoney yell from the alley, "We can't miss the bus, let's go."

Aw, hell, maybe she had read someone else's cup, and even if she didn't, a dark cloud couldn't stop this wonderful trip. I kept up my trot and ran to pick up my buddy Butts, whose real name was Pat and had gotten his nickname from Roy Rogers' sidekick, Pat Butram, because he screwed things up a lot and had a nasally voice. Butts lived two doors down, and I caught up with him at the garbage cans, but I was really starting to feel unsure about the prospects of the day. Bridie was always positive about her readings, especially on the day of an outing. "Muddled…"
Aw, to hell with it, muddled couldn't be that bad. All that mattered now was getting on that bus before anyone in charge could change their minds. I started looking forward to the first great moment of the day

16

when, as we left the classroom and headed for the bus, we could look back at the other kids stuck in their desks, and the next pleasure would be stepping across the threshold at the front door and into the free world, the one without the nuns, and letting out a loud whoop.

This was the day that I could scream till I was hoarse and play till I was black and blue and near death. It would even be okay to die…but right after the picnic. Nothing could stand between me and this deserved reward. Butts and I hurried down the alley, knocking over a couple garbage cans along the way. Halfway to school, as we were planning the day, in between breaths and under a crystal clear but chilly morning, one little old gray cloud appeared out of nowhere. I told Butts about the muddled tea leaves.

"What could possibly go wrong?" he said in his nasally voice.

"We won't let one little gray cloud stop us, will we, Butts?"

"Not on your life," he guaranteed. Butts' assurance made me feel a little better…just a little.

We got to school in time and linked up with the other soldiers of Christ, warming our arms up amid the diesel fumes of the school bus. The hum of the engines was like symphonic arias, filling the pauses between our ecstatic cries of excitement. Between each toss, we'd look over to the school doors to see if they were opening. In just a few short minutes, we'd all be sailing out to Elysium though past experience had taught us that nothing was a lock until we were clear of any nun's reach.

Today, a right turn at Oak Park Avenue and sliding across North Avenue would be our lock-in point and when the whoops would get really loud. We'd be free, and there'd be no going back. Even then we'd still check the rear windows for a screaming nun chasing the bus. As we warmed up our arms, playing catch on the lawn just outside the school doors, I got a bit saddened looking at my classmates in school garb who weren't going, but then I reminded myself that today was my treat for seeing my duty to Jesus and performing it in a timely and dedicated manner. No more sympathy for others left behind: this was *my* day.

The heavy, mosaic front door of the school began to open, and my heart started beating faster as I knew our departure grew close. I took my eye off the ball and dropped the next toss. No problem. I grabbed the damp ball from the dew-laden grass and cocked my arm to fire one back when a collective huge whoop started in response to the opening school door. Our escape was at hand. We threw our arms in the air and screamed harder. The whoop reached a crescendo, reversed and began to abate as Sr. Anna Lee poked her head out of the door and began to scan the crowd with her beady and accusatory eyes. The whoop was now a calendo inching toward expiration and then...silence. Her executing look had just sucked the wind from our bubble of excitement. But bubbles are designed to die a quick death.

Why wasn't she opening the door and letting us in? Did Bradley forget his homework again?

No, Bradley could never command the size of this stage. Anna Lee was after a bigger fish and a chance at mass compliance. Her glare scanned the crowd until it landed straight upon my head, and I sidestepped to see if it was me she was after. The glare followed.

"Oh boy," I thought. I remembered the one lone gray cloud in the teacup and Bridie's admonishment. I couldn't imagine what Sister Anna Lee was after and then I saw her index finger beckon me in with an ominous "Mr. Brennan." My name, with that "Mr." in front, was the gravest, most chilling and isolating thing that I ever heard… gravest and most chilling because there was always catastrophe at their end, especially without my first name. Dread filled my countenance, Sister Anna Lee was no fan of mine, and every chance she got to prick my puff she took. Anna Lee had a small, sallow face, her eyes forever narrowed in suspicion. I shuffled my way inside like

Duffacy at the hospital, trying to delay the inevitable as long as possible, stopped and stood before the great inquisitor, wondering how and why the axe would fall this time. The heavy door shut with a thud behind me like someone slamming a coffin lid on a despised relative.

The hallway was empty except for Sister Anna Lee and me, like Jesus and one of his souls on Judgment Day. She stood erect, hands clasped below her belt with a frigid and piercing look. Well, actually there was a trace of delight too, right at the corners of her mouth.

"Yes, Sister?" I popped my glove with my right fist, trying to hide my fears, pretending her face was in the pocket. There was no way I was going to use her whole name.

"You, sir," she started, "Missed Mass in February and once in December, and in good conscience and because it wouldn't be fair to the other servers who haven't missed, I must deny your attendance at the picnic today." She puffed her chest out, smirked and

21

raised her heels in symphony and lowered them slowly, as if to make the pain last. If she had stabbed me in the heart, she would have been kinder.

"But, Sister, those were snow days, and my route took extra time." My right hand left the glove, and both hands fell to my sides, lifeless. The glove slid off my hand and fell to the cold, marble tiles below. The thud was all that filled the deadly silence. Tears welled in my eyes. I knew the dye had been cast and nothing would change this inquisitor's sentence.

"You should have gotten up earlier," she said, assuming we knew the weather forecast.

"But, Sister, I didn't know it was going to snow," I begged. "We don't have a tellie."

"A commitment is a commitment, and I don't tolerate excuses," she argued, turning the knife in me one more rotation. "And when you do serve, your attention is wanting."

"Can't argue that one," I thought.

My tears flowed, and my breath came in gasps because I knew it was over. There would be no Altar

Boy Picnic for me today. I mustered every ounce of courage to make one more plea and ask for some mercy, but my lips were quivering and unresponsive, my breath short, and nothing came out. Numb from her edict, I dropped my head and inched down the hallway, like Duffacy, and stopped at the threshold of my classroom and took one last look back at Anna Lee and my solitary glove lying on the tile floor.

Anna Lee kicked the glove to the side. My pain doubled, but I was too weakened to put up any fight. I found my desk in the empty room and collapsed into the chair and cried and gasped. Nothing entered my mind but the sheer cruelty of Anna Lee's actions. I tried to think of someway to… but her dominance and my catatonic state wouldn't let me. It was over. I would be left with the undeserving today. With one cruel and incisive edict, all of my allegiance and service to God had been in vain.

The bell rang, and the other kids filed into the room laughing, pushing and shoving like usual, until they saw me slumped in my desk in a state of total shock. Their quick pace turned to a Duffacy crawl, their laughter turned to silence and their gazes to stares. Everyone was stunned by my uncontrollable tears. Forgetting their manners, they all just stared at Anna Lee's latest and favorite victim, slouched in his desk.

"In your desks," Anna Lee commanded, reasserting her control. And all the kids jumped and filed into their seats. It seemed like eternity, but finally the bus driver came to the door to collect the responsible altar boys.

"Gentlemen," he cried out, and in unison the good boys all rose and began to exit. Out of pure desperate hope, I started to lift myself out of my desk, caught Anna Lee's glare and slumped back. For sure it was over now. When the last champion of Christ cleared the door, I filled the air with one last wail. Butts heard the desperate cry and came back, stopped in the doorway and cast a glance that said, "I'm sorry," knowing that he'd miss his catcher today. Anna Lee sat on the edge of her desk with her arms folded, delighting in my pain. I would be left alone with Murphy, Bradley and fifteen girls, all wishing they could take me in their arms and dab my tears.

Word spread fast of Anna Lee's latest execution and got back to Bridie at Cloonmore. I was still crying and breathless when she walked through the classroom door, her head cocked and lip curled. There was complete silence except for my singular sobs. She recognized no one until her gaze circled the room and stopped at my gravesite. The teachers had switched classes by then, and I've often wondered where Sister Anna Lee would have been deposited had she been there.

Mrs. Wright looked at Bridie and with a shrug of her shoulders recognized the sheer cruelty and lunacy of the moment. Bridie, with a jerk of her head summoned me and I, still numb and sobbing uncontrollably, shuffled toward her and walked straight into her open arms and a big hug. The hug didn't last long, but it didn't have to. Her farm-girl grip infused me with instant comfort. Out the door we went and down the street we walked with her arm around my shoulder. Each step allowed me deeper breaths and by the time we got to the food store, I was beginning to think I might live through the pain and shock. There, Bridie ordered me up a fresh chocolate donut and chilled chocolate milk. Life started to be good again as I downed the donut in between my last few tears.

"Come on, Sean, we'll have our own picnic today," were the first words she spoke. We hopped on the elevated train, Bridie gave me the window seat and we headed downtown. The sound of the metal wheels on the tracks and the fleeting roof tops disappearing into the past massaged our thoughts and entranced our mood.

As I stared out the window, still in a daze, she grabbed my hand in hers and said, "There's two things I'd like you to take from this, Sean...actually, three. Number one, you can recover from anything given the resolve, and a hop in your step tomorrow will kill her glee. Number two, no sin is greater than gaining happiness from another's misfortune. And number three, you don't need such drama to get a choco out of me."

A new sweatshirt with my favorite "Aparicio" printed on the back, a hamburger deluxe from the Silver Diner and the latest cowboy movie at the State Theatre filled the afternoon and completed our picnic, all without a single ant. When we came out of the movie, the sky opened and cracked and rain started to come down, and I hoped that the boys had gotten their baseball game in at the picnic and were now sliding in the mud. Doctor Bridie had saved the day again with her favorite remedy; a little distraction and a new thought.

When we got back, as we walked from the train and headed down Oak Park Avenue toward home, she reached down and grabbed my hand, squeezed it as I looked up and she gave me her softest Irish wink.

"Don't ever let a meanie ruin your day," she said.

I responded with a skip and then another. I had that same hop in my step the next day when I went to school. Fixed and focused, I sauntered into the room with my head held high, greeted Sister Anna Lee with, "Good morning, Sister"—I still wouldn't use her whole name—and sat at my desk garbed in my new White Sox sweatshirt. I lifted the top of my desk to pull out my English book and found my catcher's mitt with a note in the pocket, "We missed you, eight passed balls."

I snickered and looked over at Butts and then straight into Sister Anna Lee's eyes with a resolve that appeared to upset even her. I knew then that no one can get you down unless you let them and that, most of all, an ounce of Bridie's potion and power was too much for a handful of anyone's evil.

Bridie had ridden to the rescue again using her usual love and magical wisdom. She had soothed my trauma and instilled in me a new resolve to perform at school and on the altar like never before. In an ironic way Anna Lee's vengeance had made me a better person… but not too good as I still found a way to sneak in the gym, knock over a few garbage cans and launch a few spitballs.

Anna Lee's reputation had taken a hit because her actions were just too cruel for anybody to justify. Sr. Michael, the principal, was one of the good nuns and knew the line between abject discipline and having a heart. I can only think that Michael felt like she owed me one and laid in wait till an opportunity presented itself.

It was December, and midnight Mass on Christmas Eve was just around the corner. Four altar boys were needed, one from each class, fifth, sixth, seventh and eighth. The call came from the cloth-covered speaker tucked in the front corner of the room during morning announcements.

"Would Sean Brennan please come down to the office?" Sister Michael beckoned over the Discipline Intercom. The usual taunts, whispers and speculations rang out.

"He's snatched another choco," from Reno.

29

"Forgot his homework again," from Haeger.

"Caught kissing again," from a jealous admirer.

It was always great to see everyone's confused expressions. Was it jail time or juice time? I looked to Anna Lee to get my release nod, and Anna Lee, sensing that Michael was throwing me a bone, reluctantly gave it to me and off to the principal's office I trotted. I was pretty sure this wouldn't be punishment, because I had been a good boy lately...well, mostly. I slipped into the principal's office and all signs seemed fine. The bane of my existence, the hulking Albanian janitor, Anton, who'd caught me stealing the chocolate milk, was nowhere to be seen...I approached the altar-like wooden desk that partially hid the tall and lanky Sister Michael.

"Well, Sean, you haven't appeared on my blotter lately, and I'm always one to give someone a second chance. How does midnight Mass sound to you?"

I was breathless and tongue-tied. I had just been offered the plum duty of the whole year.

"Midnight Mass?" I stammered.

"In one week," she said. "You best start getting prepared. That is, of course, you agree to serve."

I wiggled my cheeks and swished my tongue, trying to build some moisture in my mouth "Yes, Sister, I'm your man."

"Good," she said. "You're rounding into a fine lad."

I am?

When I went home, the screen door slammed behind me, and I yelled out. "Ma, I'm serving midnight Mass!"

Bridie came running around the kitchen corner; she was never far from the kitchen.

"Oh, Bejesus! Oh, Bejesus! Oh, Bejesus!" She reached down and wrapped her arms around my waist and lifted me in the air and swung me around.

"How'd ya pull this one off?"

"She had that, 'I owe you one' look' on her face and then said that I was turning into a fine lad."

"She did?"

"I couldn't believe it either."

For the next week, I practiced every night with the Father and other altar boys on my specific duties. The whole experience had my brain in a whirl, and when they told me that I was to swing the incense on the visiting relics, my knees knocked.

Relics?

Christmas Eve arrived, and Bridie and Pops couldn't have been prouder. Bridie ran up and down the block to find a camera to enshrine the moment in posterity. Mary Mahoney came through, and with the whole family and a few neighbors standing on the porch and crowding the stairs, Bridie pushed the flash button on her box camera and created a memory. The look on my face will go un-interpreted, much as the Mona Lisa's, and open to speculation: wisp of smile or smirk?

"My God, he looks like Jesus himself," Mary uttered to Bridie.

The night descended. The moon and our excitement rose like the expectations of a Roman coronation. And I got nervous---- with theological stage fright. In the sacristy, the room behind the altar, where the performers prepared, I paced, rehearsing my duties and occasionally peeking out through the round window on the sacristy door at the expanding crowd. The church was in full regalia, with bunting and cloaked statues, flowers and candlelight and puffy cushioned chairs for the hierarchy. I finally spotted Bridie and Pops in the fourth row, which was good seating for them because they were always late and usually landed in the back. And as each moment passed, I got a little more nervous.

"Hey, Staunton," I asked the eighth-grade altar boy with the thick glasses, "Where's the relics?"

"On the side, you dope."

"Gee, thanks."

The clock struck twelve, and the church bells pealed like gongs from heaven announcing the second coming. Everyone in church slid to the edge of their seats in expectation and then rose as the full entourage emerged from the sacristy door. It was like a courtroom when the judge announces himself. In front were three of the altar boys, including me, walking abreast, two on the sides holding a tall candle with Staunton in the middle holding the crucifix. We were followed by the main priest and, behind him, the other dignitary priests all garbed in long flowing robes and mitered hats fit for kings. It was a sight to behold.

Along our procession, I sneaked a look at the beaming Bridie and proud Pops. The Mass unfolded with bells and readings and blessings and hymns. And then the church went silent, and nothing happened, and everyone began to twist and turn, and finally Staunton whispered, "The incense, the relics."

"What relics?" I whispered.

"Now?" I was panicking.

"Now!" Staunton commanded.

I rose and retrieved the incense at a pace even Duffacy would be proud of, rehearsing my duties…what duties. I swung the thurible buying some time and to make sure the chain was free. And then I remembered something Bridie had once said in the kitchen.

"How old is that old Father Duffacy?" I asked.

"Aw, Bejesus, he's a relic."

"Okay," I thought, "Now I understand. Here goes."

Full of new found confidence and wearing my most solemn expression, I paraded over to the dignitaries, each priest older than the next, and gave them all a good incensing. All three waved their hands to disperse the smoke and let out a couple of coughs. I returned to my spot as proud as any Pope after a blessing.

"The relics!" hissed Staunton.

"Got 'em," I whispered.

The Mass continued and ended on a high note with the whole congregation singing "Hallelujah." I felt exhilarated. We paraded off of the altar the same way we'd come in, slowly and with a deep sense of protocol. And when we were finally inside the sacristy and the door closed behind us, I let out a deep breath, and Staunton let out with a, "You dope! The relics are the Saints' bones in the small, glass case. You don't incense live people, only dead ones!"

I was crushed. And I looked it. "Weren't the relics over there somewhere?"

One of the older dignitaries stepped over and put his arm on my shoulder and said, "Yes, they were over there, and I've always loved the smell of incense."

I ripped off my altar boy garb and raced down the stairs from the sacristy, again taking the last three with a leap looking for some kind of comfort somewhere. I felt like a wild wind, free from the fetters of prescribed duty, and turned and found Bridie and Pops. Bridie threw her arms around me and said, "If there was ever an angel on Earth, I'm holding him, how about some bacon and eggs?"

"It's all I want for Christmas!"

The three of us walked home in silence, embracing each other in the frigid night. At home, the party started round the kitchen table, where every party started at Cloonmore. The whole clan was there by now laughing and chiding my last mishap. Bridie broke out the cast iron skillet, and before long, the kitchen was filled with the smell of frying bacon, basting eggs and steeping tea. Bridie made the eggs the Irish way—sunny side up, basting them by softly spooning the bacon grease over the yolk.

"You know, Sean, I was wondering how the dignitaries felt about getting doused with incense?" It was Pops, spearing my yolk.

And as Bridie spooned a perfectly basted egg on my plate, "Sure, don't the old boys have one foot in the grave and the other on a banana peel...It's never a bad idea to get a head start."

I turned and looked out the window.

"It's snowing!"

It was all perfect then... My maiden Midnight Mass, crisp bacon, golden eggs, warm, buttered Irish soda bread, a spot of tea....and now the white blanketed night.

Merry Christmas.